Time Wasters/ Time Savers

61 Ways to Beat the Clock

Dr. Richard G. Neal

Time Wasters/Time Savers: 61 Ways to Beat the Clock

® 1994 by Dr. Richard G. Neal

Printed in the United States of America
ISBN: #0-910170-64-9

For more information or to purchase additional copies contact:
ASBO International
11401 North Shore Drive, Reston, Virginia 22090; 703/478-0405

About this Book

This book concerns specific time wasters and specific time savers. By avoiding the time wasters, you automatically save time. Or, to put it another way, the reverse of a time waster is a time saver. The 20 time wasters listed in this book are not abstract concepts. They are exact and real impediments to using time efficiently; and, by recognizing and avoiding these worst time wasters, you can improve time management materially, both personally and professionally.

Following the 20 worst time wasters are the 40 best time savers, all of which are practical and easy to use. No records, forms or special training are needed to implement these tactics. And, since the suggested 40 best time savers are in addition to the 20 worst time wasters, the book provides 60 of the most effective ways to use time efficiently.

I use all of these time-use tactics regularly, and, along with other strategies, they have formed the basis of numerous seminars I have offered.

Table of Contents

The *Nature* of *Time*

H ow many times have you heard an employee or colleague complain: "I just don't have enough time"? How
many times have you, yourself, run out of time before completing a task as well as you would like? How many times has your
job taken time away from your personal life due to lack of
proper time management?

A number of research projects have shown that most
administrators do not manage time to the fullest efficiency.
Administrators are generally intelligent, energetic and

committed to their jobs. Given these basic characteristics, administrators can improve their overall efficiency, while simultaneously finding more time for themselves, through better time management. This book provides practical suggestions that any administrator can use immediately.

Beginning with the first day of using these suggestions, the typical manager should begin to see results. By the end of one month, any administrator using these tactics to manage time should experience considerable improvement in his or her ability to handle the job. None of the suggestions requires any special skill or effort. Most of them can be used simply by deciding to use them. Try them and see!

How do you spend your time?

There are 8,760 hours in a year.
- We sleep about 2,920 hours each year.
- We work on the job about 1,800 hours each year.
- We spend about 300 hours in personal grooming each year.
- We use about 540 hours per year for eating.
- We spend about 500 hours each year on transportation.

That means out of 8,760 hours each year, only 2,700 are left "free." But how much of that time is actually "free" for most people? After sleeping, working, commuting and grooming, many people still have obligations to care for the inside of their homes, to fix up the outside of their homes, to care for children, and to perform other chores which must be done, leaving little "free" time for many of us. How much time, then, do each of us actually have each day, each week, each month or each year to do what we want to do? The answer to this question is often found in how well you manage time.

Naturally, the hours presented above can vary substantially from person to person. They are meant only to be averages for underscoring the fact that most people have limited "free" time. And the way to increase "free" time is through the use of easily applied timesaving tactics.

What is time?

Time is a very complex and abstract phenomenon. At the end of this sentence, stop, without reading further. Take a few minutes to try to define what time is — without using the word, time, in your definition.

If you tried this short exercise to define time, you probably found it to be exceedingly difficult.

Actually, time is the period between two events during which something exists, happens or acts.

During any period of time, humankind, the world and the universe experience changes, but time itself cannot be changed. Only some of the events which take place within time can be changed. For example, although you can "save" time by eating while you work, you are still subjected to the inexorable passage of time. Time is a fixed thing. It cannot be lengthened; it cannot be shortened. *Only the events under our control* can be speeded up or slowed down.

Time is very important because it is one of only four basic elements for us to work with in our lives. Those four elements are space, energy, materials and time. *Space* gives us room within which to work. For example, in order to conduct our lives, we must be able to move from one place to another. *Energy* gives us the power to make things happen. For example, the sun, the original source of all our energy, gives us energy in the form of food and fuel. The *materials* of the earth give us the basic ingredients we need in order to live. For example, water, soil and air are the basic materials upon which our lives are built. And then, we have *time,* the fourth element of the cosmos. Without time there could be nothing else. Time, then, is the ultimate element within which all existence takes place.

Although you can enhance your life by increasing the use of space, energy and materials, how effectively these three resources are used is determined greatly by how well you use time. After all, we will all die; and, frankly, we will all die soon, at least in relation to the infinite duration of the universe. In terms of the universe, our lives are but fleeting moments. Consequently, we must learn to use well what little time is left to us in our present form here on earth.

Which raises a very important question: How do you wish to spend the rest of your life? After all, there isn't much time left. Are you now living to die, or are you dying to live? Is this the beginning of the end of your life, or is this the beginning of the rest of your life? Is your life filled with problems, or is it filled with opportunities? You have only the time between now and when you die. How will you use this precious and finite resource?

In answering these important questions, most of us will find that working for a living must still go on. Few of us will ever find total freedom to do as we wish. Most of us will conclude that continuing to work until retirement is necessary. For those people, this book offers a number of very useful tactics for getting more done within a fixed period of time.

Why do people "save" time?

Most people intuitively recognize that time should not be "wasted." But what is "wasted" time? Wasted time is that period during which events take place which are not worthwhile—from our own point of view. Waiting for a bus to go to work or standing in a queue at the post office is viewed by some as wasted time. Watching an unenjoyable movie or an inane television program is a waste of time. A useless meeting is a waste of time.

We all know when we have wasted time. We have wasted time when we are involved in something which does not contribute to the fulfillment of our enjoyment or responsibilities.

The opposite of wasting time is "saving" time. But time cannot be "saved." Time marches on, and there is no force on earth which can stop its consistent and persistent passage. When we "save" time, we are really only manipulating the events under our control so that these events use as little time as possible.

Wouldn't it be great if time could be saved like money and put into a bank to be used later when we want it? But time cannot be saved.

Time steadily disappears, and it cannot be retrieved. Time is the ultimate prison of life. Perhaps if we could achieve immortality, we could have some relief from time. True, immortality would give us more time for our lives, but even immortality would not stop the passage of time.

What is "saved" time?

As has been stated previously, time cannot be "saved." So what is "saved" time? "Saved" time is time diverted from other tasks in order to do things we want to do, or are required to do, for which there would not otherwise be time. In other words, we use our time efficiently on Friday morning so we can leave the office on Friday afternoon to play golf. Or we use our time efficiently on Friday morning so we can be ready for an important staff meeting on Friday afternoon. In the first case, the incentive is to obtain time to have fun. In the second, the incentive to save time is to be able to complete a required task on the job.

In order to save time, there must be some purpose. The purpose can be to have extra time to relax. The purpose can be to have time for a part-time job. The purpose can be to have time to fulfill family responsibilities. Or the purpose of saving time can be to accomplish more on the job in order to obtain a pay raise or a promotion.

Without some purpose for saving time, little time will be saved. Therefore, an important prerequisite for saving time is the adoption of objectives and goals for your life. For those who set short-range objectives and long-range goals, there is an automatic commitment to saving time because such people recognize that time is limited and that the likelihood of achieving their goals can be enhanced through effective use of time.

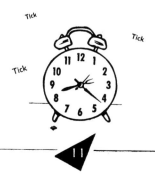

The 20 Worst Time Wasters

B efore we list the specific suggestions for saving time, let's look at the main causes of wasted time. Not every reader will be able to avoid or correct every time waster listed. But when viewed as a whole, there's something in this list for every administrator. The chief time wasters are:

1. Time seen as having little value

Have you ever known a person who seems to have all the time in the world? These are the people who will always stop and listen to anybody who wants to talk. These are the people who never seem to be going anywhere or who never appear to have anything in particular to do. Although there are some people who can allow time to pass in this manner, it's not a life-style suited to the busy administrator who has deadlines to meet and jobs to complete.

Therefore, the greatest time waster is a lack of appreciation for the importance of time as a resource. People such as those described above seem to view time as endlessly available. Such people fail to recognize that time moves relentlessly and cannot be stopped or slowed. Such people appear to be drifters on the ocean of time, directed by the powers of the wind and currents of the sea. Such people are seldom achievers and let their lives pass by with little of value having been accomplished.

2. Poor health

How much efficiency do you lose in your life because of illness or because you just don't feel well? For many people, illnesses and lack of vitality are serious impediments to productive use of their time. Granted, not everyone can be in perfect health, but everyone can improve their health and vitality to some extent. Health problems caused by smoking can be corrected if the smoker has the desire to do so. Health problems caused by intoxicants and addictive drugs can be corrected if one has the will power.

Poor eating habits can be a source of poor health and lack of vitality, but this behavior, too, can be corrected *if* you decide that health and vitality are more important than the temporary pleasure associated with excessive eating.

Good natural food, light exercise and adequate rest, coupled with the proper mental attitude, are the prerequisites to good health, and none of these requirements demands an excessive use of time. As a matter of fact, proper eating takes less time than excessive eating, and light exercise can be incorporated into your daily activities without taking any extra time. As far as sleeping is concerned, good food and light exercise make less sleep possible, especially if you learn how to relax during the day to conserve energy. In summary, most people have the wherewithal within themselves to improve significantly their health, with no additional investment of time or money. The end result is less loss of time for work and play.

3. Egotism

Many people have a need for attention. Often these people have a tendency to be self-centered and consider only their selfish interests. Such people are egotists. In other words, they are not in control of their egos. Often such people spend a portion of each day on the job satisfying their own egos through a variety of convoluted behavior patterns. They talk just to hear themselves talk. They socialize too much in order to talk about themselves. Their main motive on the job appears to be to prove how important they are, rather than to concentrate on getting a task done well.

Those who must have attention and constantly prove their superiority and importance have a daily burden which more stable people do not need to carry. The constant use of egotistical behavior consumes a lot of time, time which inevitably is taken away from other, more important, tasks. Therefore, you should check your motives regularly during contact with employees and colleagues to determine to what extent time is being spent in satisfying your own ego rather than in completing a task promptly.

4. Lack of objectives and goals

Every administrator should have long-range goals and short-range objectives. Administrators should know exactly what they plan to achieve each day, each week, each month and each year. As soon as these goals and objectives are set, you must then develop a strategy to achieve these goals and objectives. Inevitably, such a strategy must include a timeline along which certain objectives must be met in order to arrive at the appointed goal by the established deadline.

For example, if you are scheduled for a meeting from 1:30 p.m. until 5:00 p.m., you must organize the morning in order to complete the important tasks for that day by around 12:30 p.m. in order to have time for lunch. If you must have a comprehensive report ready by the end of the week, a plan must be established which calls for the orderly completion of tasks which result in the report being finished by the end of the week.

In other words, when deadlines are established for the achievement of goals, you must prepare to cause a series of events to take place within a specified period of time. The more complex the goals, the more valuable time becomes. For people who have nowhere to go and no goals to achieve, time has little significance. But for people who have jobs to complete and deadlines to beat, time becomes a precious possession. Such people soon learn by experience that time cannot be wasted.

5. Poor decisions from above

The main function of managers is to organize and supervise the work of people under their direction. Therefore, poor organization and supervision by a manager can cause wasted time by subordinates. Generally speaking, the higher the organizational rank of administrators, the more important their decisions. For example, a decision by an army general to invade enemy territory is more important than a decision by a supply sergeant to delete fresh milk from the chow line.

As a rule, the impact of an administrator's decision is correlated with the number of people in the department and the amount of budgetary funds the administrator controls. Naturally, there are some exceptions to this rule, but the point is this: Regardless of an administrator's position on the organizational chart, decisions made by the administrator affect the work of that department's personnel; therefore, poor decisions by this person often cause time to be wasted by subordinates.

Poor planning, supervision and direction from above can affect the smallest office as well as the largest office. The supervisor who cannot dictate a letter correctly the first time wastes supervisory and secretarial time each time the letter is redone. The chief executive who calls an all-staff meeting just to make a routine announcement wastes a vast amount of expensive time. Therefore, all managerial decisions you make which require time from your subordinates should be made with high regard for how much time will be required to implement such decisions.

6. Poor equipment and supplies

I have worked in a number of offices where it was impossible to obtain immediate word processor and computer repair, causing secretaries (and their bosses) to waste time unnecessarily. For most secretaries, the word processor is an indispensable tool, and, without it, work simply cannot be performed. An organization which cannot keep operable equipment available at all times for *all* employees is an organization in need of new managers.

All business operations need equipment and supplies, and, when the equipment is broken and the supplies are missing, time is wasted. The broken copy machine, the inoperable word processor, the missing collator and the downed computer can rob the organization of time vital to achieving its mission. The best rule is: any piece of equipment worth purchasing is worth keeping in working order at all times.

7. Inability to establish priorities

Each act that an administrator performs creates a certain impact on the organization. For example, a decision to change the agency letterhead sets into motion a whole series of events, from the design of the new letterhead, to the printing of the new stationery, to the distribution of the new supplies. Whereas, a decision to move a filing cabinet in an office would have limited impact on the work of the organization.

The importance of a decision is determined by its relative impact on the mission of the agency and its relative demand on the resources of the agency. For example, a decision to determine the color of binders for regulations would have little impact on the mission or resources of the agency, but a decision to rewrite the regulations of the agency could have an inestimable impact on the mission and resources of the organization.

The problem with some administrators is, however, that they can't differentiate between the relative importance of decisions. Some administrators will spend more time arguing over the color of the binders than the decision to rewrite the regulations. It is this inability to set a priority on decisions which can result in untold amounts of wasted time.

8. Negative working environment

I once worked in a bureaucracy where the leadership had become more concerned with political intrigue and personal vendettas than it was with carrying out the mission of the organization. The working environment in that particular situation was permeated with suspicion, fear and disrespect. As a result, vast energy and endless hours were dissipated in gossip, malingering and self-protection. The management staff was so intimidated that no one would make a decision or take responsibility for any action. They became so divided that more time was invested in interoffice turf warfare than in legitimate management functions. As a result of the negative environment, an inestimable amount of time was wasted. To avoid such a deplorable situation, every manager should establish a working environment that fosters security, trust and respect so that employees can devote their energies full-time to the business of the organization.

9. Unclear chain of command

E very organization needs to be structured so that its members understand the hierarchy for making decisions. Each employee should have only one boss. All recommendations should go to that person, and all directions to the employee should come from that same person. Failure to adhere to this simple fundamental rule allows bypassing of superiors, fosters disloyalties and diffuses accountability. As a result, there is a breakdown in the management integrity of the organization, and much more time is needed to get things done than is the case where a clear chain of command exists and is understood by all members of the agency.

10. Staff turnover

According to the concept discussed in the book *Theory Z,* employees are a capital investment of an organization, and, as such, they should not be lost to the organization. According to this view of employees, every reasonable effort should be made to retain employees and enhance their job performance. According to the author, Professor William G. Ouchi, high staff turnover would likely be a sign of poor management because it would mean that the agency was losing a large portion of its investment as employees leave.

Almost all employees perform jobs which required some degree of training and expertise. When these people leave that employer, they take with them all of the skills that were learned on the job. As a general rule, the replacement must relearn those same skills, which takes precious time away from the continuing needs of the organization.

Although much turnover among American workers can be attributed to factors other than job dissatisfaction, a significant amount of employee turnover does take place because of job-related problems. Where such turnover is allowed to continue with no effort to reduce it, the employer is probably losing expensive time which otherwise could be saved. To minimize this loss of time, you should analyze the reasons for employee resignation in order to take appropriate corrective actions. By reducing employee turnover, you can take an important step in avoiding another serious time waster.

11. Spur of the moment meetings

How many times have you organized your day carefully, only to have it disorganized by your boss calling an unscheduled meeting? How many times have *you* called a meeting of your employees without any reasonable advance notice? Such unscheduled meetings not only disrupt the planned day for those who must attend, but they also have a ripple effect. For example, Mr. Jones is required to attend an unscheduled meeting, but Mr. Jones had already scheduled a meeting of his staff which he must cancel, a meeting which may have been very difficult to arrange. Although emergency meetings are by their very nature unscheduled and are, therefore, justified, in too many instances the unscheduled meeting is held simply because the administrator was poorly organized and viewed the time of staff to be of limited value.

To minimize the loss of time due to unscheduled meetings, you should call meetings only when a meeting is the best method for accomplishing a given task. If meetings are a necessary part of the agency's operation, then they should be scheduled in such a manner that unscheduled meetings become unnecessary. Unfortunately, however, some administrators violate this simple rule because they seem to think that anything they want is automatically more important than the collective activities of their subordinates.

12. Excessive coffee breaks

Socialization and relaxation on the job are acceptable—in moderation. Carried to excess, however, coffee breaks can create a number of developments which waste time on the job. Excessive coffee breaks are not only time wasters for the coffee drinkers, but they set a bad example for other employees who may follow the lead set by others. Furthermore, some employees cannot afford to take coffee breaks because of their job demands; consequently, these people may resent those who seem to be on a perpetual break. Although coffee breaks can provide an opportunity for employees to get to know one another and thereby develop more productive working relationships, excessive coffee breaks can lead to social relationships back on the job which waste time. In order to minimize the coffee break as a time waster, you should monitor your own rest breaks and those of your subordinates.

13. Red tape

All of us have had to endure "red tape" some time in our lives. But exactly what is "red tape"? As used by most people, red tape is the requirement to complete tasks which are not needed to accomplish an overall objective. Government agencies, more so than private companies, seem to create red tape. There are many reasons for this phenomenon, all of which are rooted in differences between private enterprise and government service.

When a government agency requires that a two-page form be completed in order to requisite an extra trash pick up, that's likely to be red tape. This red tape usually results from imposing excessive ancillary or unrelated demands on a process to achieve an objective. For example, when a parent is required to complete a long, complicated form in order to apply for scholarship aid on the basis of need, the form will likely call for information that is not specifically needed to determine if the applicant qualifies. The form will likely seek information which will be used in an accounting study for some government agency. And although the government agency may have a need for such information (from its point of view), the individual applicant will probably view irrelevant questions as examples of red tape and a waste of time.

There are many reasons for red tape. Quite often the reason is based upon the fact that there are a few people in any organization who cannot be trusted. As a result, all employees must complete forms and engage in activities designed to minimize the risk of dishonest actions by the few. Regardless of the reason for it, wherever red tape exists, it should be viewed critically because it is a potential source of wasted time.

14. Rivalries

Although some competition between employees and between departments within an agency is healthy, excessive competition can develop into harmful rivalries. Each manager, from the chief executive to the first-line supervisor, should develop a perception to detect latent human relations problems in the department which might grow into unhealthy rivalries. Where an administrator is responsible for more than one department, steps should be taken to preclude competition which may be harmful to any department under that person's supervision. The chief executive can make a real contribution to interdepartmental relationships by setting a tone of cooperation and by making it clear in various ways that rivalries between departments and individuals will not be tolerated. Government service is a human service. It is not a profit-making organization, and, as such, all employees of the agency should view themselves as members of one team.

Where rivalries are allowed to exist, there is an inevitable waste of time. For example, I was associated with an organization where the chief executive relished competition between staff members. He thought that such an environment would foster greater efficiency. What he didn't realize, though, was that the competition which he fostered resulted in a lack of cooperation between the various departments, thus diminishing, not increasing, efficiency. So much time was spent on advancing selfish departmental goals, that little time was left for overall agency goals.

15. Lack of authority

In contrast to private industry, the decision-making process in government is more diffused. Part of the cause for this diffusion can be traced to the absence of authority where responsibility is assigned. As a general rule, any employee given responsibility for a task must be given the authority to accomplish the task. Failure of responsibility and authority to go hand-in-hand can result in a significant impediment of overall work efficiency.

For example, the common practice in public school districts is to hold the building principal responsible for the cleanliness of the school building. But in a number of school districts, the individual building principal has limited authority over the custodians and limited power to obtain cleaning supplies and equipment. In such a situation, how can the building principal be held accountable for building cleanliness? If the principal is held accountable for keeping the school clean, the principal must have direct supervisory authority over the custodians and must have a reasonable budget to purchase supplies and equipment.

Failure to assign authority with responsibility results in duplication, performance voids, buck-passing and other practices which waste time. Therefore, you should carefully review the job descriptions of assigned employees to assure that each has the authority to accomplish the tasks assigned to him or her.

16. Action without thought

Many decisions of government are very complex matters, whether they are policy decisions of the government body or administrative decisions of the executive staff. Decisions generally result in something happening or something ceasing to happen. In either case, decisions have an impact on the operation of the agency. The more important the decision, the greater the impact on the organization. But whether decisions are minor or major, they should be prepared for as carefully as time and resources permit. Although the ability to make decisions quickly is generally a quality admired in executives, quick decisions can be expensive, if they are the wrong decisions.

All administrators have experienced occasions when they made a wrong decision because it was made in haste. Through this experience, most veteran administrators recognize that no decision is simple. Although speed may be a virtue in making emergency decisions, successful administrators are measured by the degree to which they carefully analyze all factors related to an issue before making a decision. Making a decision without such careful consideration results in expending time pursuing the wrong objectives.

17. Failure to identify the problem

Running a school system is largely a process of solving a continuous stream of problems. The first step in solving any problem is to identify the problem. Failure to identify the problem at the outset wastes time planning a solution to the problem; plus, it wastes time in the actual solution of the problem.

Identification of a problem can sometimes take more time than constructing a solution to the problem. This phenomenon is particularly true in government service where there are political overtones to many administrative decisions. For example, a school board may find statistics indicate that while the cost of education increases, the educational achievement of students decreases. Given this hypothetical situation, the school board may think it has discovered the "problem." But they have not discovered *the* problem; they have only discovered some facts which may not even be verified.

Suppose, however, that this mythical school board decided wrongly that the "problem" was that children were not taught to read by phonics because of political pressure by a group of parents. And suppose, as a result of this pressure, the school board embarked upon a long-range reading program which five years later produced no appreciable change in the original statistics. Wouldn't this be a tragic waste of time? Unfortunately, this hypothetical example is too often indicative of reality in the public sector, where political considerations are often more important than solving the substantive problem.

18. *Meddling policymakers*

There are several fundamental differences between private enterprise and government service which account for the better use of time in the private sector. Whereas the private sector involves private *economic* transactions, the public sector involves public *political* transactions. As a result, private enterprise is more able to devote its time specifically to its objectives. On the other hand, the nature of government is such that it must wade through a swamp of political considerations in order to achieve its objectives.

In the private sector, private companies are generally run by the managers, not by boards of directors. But in the public sector, boards of directors, e.g., school boards, city councils, etc., do play an active role in managing government services. And the nature of government is such that members of these boards are likely to be amateurs in management affairs. Furthermore, these board members are just as likely to be highly motivated by political considerations.

When members of governing bodies with limited managerial skill and considerable political motivation step out of their legitimate policy-making role and attempt to administer an agency, serious problems can be anticipated. I have been involved in a number of situations where the governing body seemed to see no distinction between the adoption of policy and the administration of policy. When policymakers attempt to administer an organization, the ultimate result is decreased efficiency, which means that significant time is being wasted. In order to minimize the possibility that such a state of affairs will develop, the superintendent and the school board should attempt to achieve a *modus operandi* regarding their respective roles, based upon the best interest of the school system. More specifically, the superintendent should take the initiative in helping board members understand their proper role through a variety of in-service programs.

19. Lost and inaccessible information

How much time does your secretary spend each day searching for needed information in the files? How often have you faced an emergency when existing information was needed, but it couldn't be located? How often has your department needed information that existed, but simply was not accessible? Wherever there is a poorly organized information storage or retrieval system, there is bound to be a significant amount of time wasted. Decisions are based upon information, and not all information can be stored in the minds of employees. Data, reports, correspondence, charts, documents, etc., all contain information which is needed by an organization in order to make good decisions. If this information is not readily accessible, much valuable time can be dissipated.

Information management is a subject appropriate for an entire book so it will not be discussed in detail here. Suffice it to say that there are many school systems which don't even have a complete set of codified policies and regulations, let alone an organized method for filing and storing information. Such organizations seem to be in a perpetual tizzy in trying to make decisions. As a result, every employee in those organizations is forced to participate in a mammoth time wasting process.

The solution? Codify the agency's policies and regulations, and establish a modern system for information storage, management and quick retrieval.

20. Failure to organize

One of the worst wasters of time is the inability or failure to organize tasks. The failure to organize your work can be due to a number of causes. The inability to differentiate between the importance of various tasks can result in more time being spent on the unimportant than the important. The failure to use delegation properly can result in the department head being inundated with work, while subordinates sit idly by. The inability to see a large job as a sequence of individual small tasks can make routine jobs difficult and protract their accomplishment. And, as has been mentioned previously, the absence of goals and objectives can cause an administrator to flounder on the job.

Whatever the cause, inability to organize is a problem so serious that, if uncorrected, it will not only waste time for the administrator, but will spread inevitably to subordinates. In some cases, the root cause of lack of organization can be so complex that a remedy is impossible. In such cases, the offender should be placed in another position more suitable to his or her abilities.

C ertainly you won't be able to keep every employee from resigning or eliminate every instance of red tape that exists in your organization. Somethings are simply beyond your control. But consistently avoiding even a few of the time wasters mentioned here will significantly reduce the amount of time lost to inefficiency in your daily activities.

Now let's look at some of the positive steps you can take to "save" time.

Tick

Tick

Tick

The 40 Best Time Savers

A lthough time cannot be "saved," the events which take place within time can be manipulated so that they take less time than otherwise would be the case. This section contains the best time savers that an administrator can use. Each one is practical and immediately usable, requiring no special training or unreasonable effort. By incorporating these tactics into your professional and personal life, there should be an immediate increase in the amount of "free" time available.

1. Double time and triple time

One way to increase achievement during a fixed period of time is to perform two or three activities at once. For example, many meetings require so little attention that the attendees can work on paper tasks while the meeting is in progress. For people who can deal with only one thought at a time, doubling up on time may be of limited value. But most competent administrators have learned to give attention to two trains of thought at one time. For example, many people can read a memorandum while listening to someone discuss another topic. Such a skill is an important asset in saving time.

I have found that eating lunch in my office provides a great deal of time which otherwise would be spent in transportation, waiting and socializing. By eating lunch in the office, you can "find" about 200 hours per year to be used as you see fit. Just think—200 hours is five work weeks! As an example of how valuable this time can be, I wrote an entire book within one year by using only my lunch period.

In addition to saving time by eating in your office, there is the double bonus of saving money and controlling your diet. By carrying your lunch, the quality of the food can be controlled better. Eating lunch in the office may not be suitable for everyone, but such a tactic can produce vast amounts of time.

The opportunities for doubling up on time are almost limitless. Some people exercise while watching television. Others complete routine paperwork while talking on the phone. And, in some cases, time can be put to triple use as I often do by listening to educational tapes and developing plans while commuting to work.

2. Impose deadlines

According to Parkinson's law, work expands to fill the time available. To avoid this common phenomenon, effective administrators set deadlines for themselves and their subordinates. By establishing a specific point in time by which a task must be completed, you are forced to place a value on time and to apportion it to the task carefully. The absence of deadlines will not only waste time, but also cause missions to fail.

The process of setting deadlines can range from the simple to the complex. Telling a secretary that a letter must by prepared by 3:00 p.m. is quite easy since there is only one deadline involved. However, setting deadlines for the completion of the agency budget is far more complex and will involve many deadlines. In establishing deadlines for complex jobs, the *final* deadline for the completion of the entire task must be determined first. All other deadlines for the subparts of the job must then be subservient to that ultimate deadline.

For example, suppose your office must prepare a report for distribution to all employees. The first step is to set a specific deadline by which all employees should have the report in their hands. From that date other deadlines are established to assure that the final deadline is met. A date must be set for the report to be printed. A deadline must be set for the report to be copy-ready for the printer. A date must be set for the final draft to be ready. A deadline must be set for the first draft of the report, and so on. With such carefully orchestrated deadlines, much time will be saved. Without such deadlines, the report will likely never materialize.

3. Delete some activities

Since time is fixed and cannot be lengthened, how we use our time is a matter of priorities. For example, do we watch television or go for a walk? The choice is a matter of priorities.

Some activities are simply a waste of time in comparison to all of the good things we could spend our time on. Therefore, some time-consuming activities in our lives should be simply eliminated. For example, a number of studies indicate that on the average, Americans spend about 35 hours each week watching television. For people who want full lives, 35 hours of watching television each week is not wise. Many people spend exorbitant amounts of time on excessive personal grooming. For example, some people spend several hundred hours each year just taking care of their hair. For people with long hair, this amount of time could be reduced by keeping their hair short. Suffice it to say that an awful lot of time (and money) is spent needlessly by an awful lot of people just dressing their hair.

4. Use creative periods

Many people claim they have special times when they are energetic and creative. Some people are early-morning people, while some are night owls. If there is a special time during the day when you feel more energetic and creative, then that period should be taken advantage of. I have found that my most productive period for writing is very early in the morning, when energy is plentiful and distractions few.

If you have an assignment which requires a high degree of concentration and creativity, you should try to reserve creative time during the day for this activity. If the creative period is late at night, then the time spent late at night can be deducted from the normal daytime hours, if acceptable to your employer. By using those creative moments, more can be achieved in a fixed period of time than otherwise would be the case. In some cases and for some people, one hour of concentrated work during a creative period late at night can be worth three hours of work in the office during the afternoon.

5. Control those worries

Fear and worry are strong emotional motivators in our lives, causing us to take necessary actions to protect ourselves. However, constant fear and worry about everything can be a serious handicap. If we worry constantly about all of the potential dangers in life, not only do we waste much time, but we paralyze our ability to think clearly and make wise decisions. The excessively fearful person seeks ways to minimize all risks, thus allowing time and opportunity to pass for fear of making a wrong decision. On the other hand, a confident person, one who seldom experiences fear, will seek out new experiences and better opportunities. This type of person seldom wastes time.

The constant presence of worry is an energy-draining burden and a time-wasting distraction. Everybody will face hardships sometime during their lives. That's an immutable reality. We can waste time worrying about those inevitabilities, or we can set these fears aside and get on with the business of living a full life.

There is no simple formula for controlling fear and worry, but this rule should help: Either take action to remove or minimize the source of fear or forget it. Or, put more poignantly in the familiar exhortation: *"Give me the strength to change the things which I can change, the serenity to live with that which I cannot change, and the wisdom to tell the difference."*

6. The tickler file

All administrators must meet deadlines themselves and assure that subordinates meet their deadlines. As discussed previously, if deadlines are not set and adhered to, much time can be forever lost. But how can you keep up with all of the various deadlines which your subordinates must meet? Simple. Set up a *tickler file*. A tickler file has thirty-one (31) folders in it—one for each day of the month. Every time a deadline of a certain date, e.g., the 21st of the month is given to a subordinate, a copy of the directive is placed in the tickler file folder marked the "21st." This is one simple tactic you can use, and it is guaranteed to save significant amounts of time. Not only that, this tactic will also free your mind of useless baggage so you can concentrate on productive enterprises.

7. Screen telephone calls

Some administrators will accept a telephone call from anybody at any time. Such a practice is a waste of valuable time. Many telephone calls consume time unnecessarily and interrupt vital work. Just because a caller wants to talk to you does not give that person an automatic right to interrupt your work at the caller's convenience.

There are several ways to avoid wasting time on unnecessary telephone interruptions. For example, a competent secretary can handle many inquiries without your help. There are many tactful ways that your secretary can inquire into the nature of the caller's business. Or some calls appropriately can be referred to a subordinate. If neither of these tactics work, your secretary can ascertain what the caller wants, and you can return the call later. Some administrators protect their time by accepting calls only at a specified time during the day, except for emergencies and high priority calls.

The telephone is an indispensable tool on the job and in our personal lives, but it must be used properly, as any special tool should be. By limiting telephone conversations to those which specifically require your personal involvement, hours of valuable extra time can be produced to use for more important work.

8. Clear instructions

M uch time is wasted on the job because many employees do not understand the directions given to them. Sometimes this occurs because the boss doesn't have a clear picture of what needs to be done. But more often than not, the confusion stems from an inability to articulate a direction clearly. Whenever a subordinate is in doubt as to what is being requested, an attempt should be made to repeat the request to you. If you doubt that the subordinate understands what is being asked, you should ask the employee to repeat the request, and, when necessary, describe how the request will be accomplished. Failure to reach a clear understanding at the outset of a task can increase the chance that time will be spent on needless tasks, while required tasks go undone.

9. Schedule appointments carefully

I once worked for a chief executive who could not (would not?) conclude appointments on time. Beginning with the first appointment in the morning, he would begin to fall behind on his appointment schedule. By lunch time, two or three people would be waiting in anger while one or two others had left in frustration. Not only was he taking too much of his own time in conferences, but he was wasting the valuable time of others who were forced to wait. Just imagine the impact that such poor control had on the overall time management of that particular agency. Not only was time wasted, but poor human relations were created.

In the case cited above, better scheduling could have helped relieve the problem. If a chief executive wants to waste time in appointments, that's the executive's business, but that person shouldn't impose the consequences of such inefficiency upon innocent others. In situations where a chief executive allows the staff to express reasonable criticism, the problem described here should be called to the attention of the offender. Where the boss discourages such constructive advice, the organization may have no choice but to endure.

10. Delegate

Some administrators seem so impressed with their own ability and so suspicious of the abilities of others that they cannot let go of any job. Although some subordinates need more direction and supervision than others, most subordinates are capable of doing an acceptable job without interference from the boss. Therefore, the basic rule in delegation is: Delegate—*the entire job!*

In my article "The Fine Art of Delegating," which appeared in the November 1992 issue of *The Executive Educator,* I discuss delegation in more detail than I am able to do here. But, in general, it helps to remember the following: In order to delegate an entire job to a subordinate, it may be necessary to transfer some authority so that the responsibility assigned to the subordinate is accompanied by the necessary clout to get the job done. In those situations where needed authority cannot be transferred to a subordinate, it may be necessary for you to intercede at appropriate times to assure that certain required acts take place.

For example, suppose that you expect your secretary to arrange all appointments. If this is actually what you want, then you should allow your secretary to arrange *all* appointments without interference. In making this assignment to your secretary at the outset, however, you should give guidelines within which to operate. You should also make it clear to your secretary that she or he is being given the authority to make decisions as to when and how long appointments should be. At that point, you should forget about making appointments and go on to other challenges.

11. Break it down

Some projects on the job are very large in scope and very complex in nature, sometimes appearing to be impossible tasks when first viewed. As has been discussed earlier, the failure to plan carefully how a task will be accomplished cannot only waste valuable time, but worse, poor planning can actually result in failure to perform the task. Some jobs seem so overpowering when viewed *in toto* that it's difficult to even know where to begin. In such cases, planning is even more imperative to avoid wasted time.

One way to conquer a difficult task is to break it down into its various parts. The individual components of a task are always simpler than the whole of the components. Once the task is broken down to its simpler parts, you have taken the first constructive step in accomplishing the assignment in avoiding wasted time.

12. The to-do list

I n the section on time wasters, the importance of goals and objectives was discussed. But goals and objectives cannot be achieved unless the administrator has a plan for *each day*. In other words, within reason, you should have a list of specific activities to be completed each day. As a general rule, the list should contain a few more items than would usually be considered a normal load. By doing this, you are forced to budget time and use other techniques of efficiency in order to complete all items on the list.

Necessity is the mother of invention, and a list of to-do items with more items than the average administrator would normally handle is the best way to prove this aphorism. By using this tactic daily, you will discover many imaginative ways to save time, in addition to those discussed in this book.

13. Handle paper only once

Following is a brief description of how to waste time dealing with routine work. An administrator receives a memorandum and reads it but can't make a decision as to what action should follow. It is placed on a stack of other materials similarly dealt with. The next day the administrator reviews the stack of papers again. This time a decision is made on a few of them, but most papers are returned to the stack. In the meantime, additional memoranda arrive which are read and placed on the stack. Day by day the stack grows. As a result, valuable time is wasted and decisions are left unmade, which in turn wastes time for others.

With only an occasional exception, I put all communications I receive in one of three separate categories on my desk. The first category is for those items which can or should be decided upon immediately. The second is for communications which should or do require action, but not immediately. The third category consists of reading material which would be advisable to read, but is not actually required reading. Materials are placed in their proper categories after a quick initial scanning. After that, the paper is handled only once, which means that a decision of some kind is made on each item. The purpose of this procedure is to keep the paper moving off my desk in an expeditious manner.

Most administrators must know how to handle paper traffic to survive, and the method described above will work for most people. It shows at a glance how far behind you are at any given time and provides a clear picture of what is pending. It moves paper off the desk daily and holds items which need further examination. Regardless of the actual method used, however, the universal rule is: *Handle it only once.*

14. Have a plan for all meetings

Many administrators are responsible for conducting numerous meetings. The potential for saving time or wasting time in these meetings is compounded in direct relation to the number of people involved. Keep in mind that five minutes wasted in a meeting of 12 people is an entire employee-hour lost. How many supervisors would allow an employee to sit for one hour doing nothing?

Making an assumption that all administrators are capable of conducting a meeting, here are some simple rules to avoid wasting time:

- Distribute a printed agenda with the times noted for each item of business.
- Identify to the group what the objective is for each item. In some cases the objective will be to provide information, while in other cases the objective may be to arrive at a group decision.
- Do not run overtime. If necessary, reschedule the meeting.
- Keep all discussion relevant to the topic under consideration.
- Require punctuality of all members.
- Have all needed materials present and ready for use.
- Try to finish early. This will provide you with "found" time, which can be applied to other activities.

In some cases, a meeting can be expedited by scheduling it before lunch or an hour before quitting time. Such deadlines will impose pressure on each participant to conserve time without any direction from the chairperson.

15. Use ad hoc committees

S ome jobs are too big for one person, too small for an entire committee, or they cut across departmental lines. In such cases, you should consider the possibility of using an ad hoc committee. Such a committee is one designed for a single purpose for a single time. An ad hoc committee is usually composed of people best suited to accomplish the objective of the special assignment, and, by matching employees with a specific task, time is used efficiently.

By way of example, let's assume that an agency head has decided that the agency should attempt to organize a recreational program for employees and gives the assignment to the personnel director. Given this hypothetical case, the personnel director would be well advised to organize an ad hoc committee to draw up recommendations. The committee should be composed of representatives from various departments of the agency. The personnel director, in keeping with advice discussed earlier in this book, should give the committee clear directions and set a deadline by which a report should be completed.

16. Establish some private time

Have you ever gone to your office on a Saturday, Sunday or holiday and discovered how much "work" you could accomplish without any distractions from telephone calls, drop-ins and appointments? If you have not had this experience, try it sometime. You'll find that you can accomplish two days' work in one, at least. For years I edited several newsletters by working only one morning each weekend. This produced at least eight hours of "found" time during the week for other jobs, or time off for recreation or personal obligations.

Some administrators have found that they can set aside some time early in the morning before official office hours for their private time. Others stay late after work. Some administrators simply reserve time on a regular basis during which they will not be disturbed except for emergencies. Whatever method is used to acquire it, however, private time can be a valuable tactic in saving time. By setting aside time to do those tasks which require privacy and concentration, you minimize the stop-and-go nature of the office routine which is very disruptive and time wasting for tasks requiring protracted concentration.

17. Keep an organized office

Ionce worked for a chief executive who allowed nothing of an obvious work-related nature to be in his office except those items which were of required utilitarian use, e.g., a desk, a chair, a telephone and a small conference table with four chairs. That was all! No decorations, no desk paraphernalia, no filing cabinet. That office reflected the man's approach to his job which was that *all* paper work should be managed by an aide.

You may not have an administrative aide, but you probably have a secretary. And, with proper guidance and delegation, a good secretary can help you organize the office so that it is a time saver, rather than a time waster. Although there are some administrators who seem able to locate needed items despite excessive clutter, on the average, an orderly office indicates an orderly administrator.

An orderly office is likely to be one where much of the paper work has been delegated to the secretary. As far as time saving is concerned, this method is quite advantageous to you as the administrator in that none of your time is lost in searching for a particular document. When material is needed, simply request your secretary to retrieve it while you continue to work on more productive enterprises. True, your secretary must take time to locate an item, but his or her time is likely to be less costly than yours.

18. Write brief letters

Some administrators waste time by writing long letters and memoranda when just a brief note or telephone call would be sufficient. Unfortunately, some correspondence which would otherwise be unnecessary is caused by a working environment of excessive fear, where the administrator feels the need to create a "paper trail" as protection from blame should something go wrong. This syndrome is indicative of an employment atmosphere which in itself is a terrible time waster, but this problem is discussed elsewhere in this book.

The point being stressed here is that written communications can be time savers or time wasters, depending upon how they are handled. If a formal memorandum or letter is necessary, then it should be as short as possible. In many cases, however, a response to a letter or memorandum can be handwritten on the original correspondence. Although some purists may find this objectionable, the technique does save time. Where the administrator is originating a written communication, a simple handwritten note may be sufficient in many cases.

I handle most written communications by using a typewriter to send brief notes, where a formal communication is not necessary. The use of the typewriter (or word processor) is not only quicker than handwritten messages, it has the added advantage of saving time for the recipient, who is spared the pain of translating indecipherable handwriting.

19. Eat light meals

As discussed elsewhere, eating at restaurants can consume time unnecessarily, and eating heavy meals, rather than light meals, adds to the actual amount of time needed for eating. Heavy meals are a time waster in an indirect way, too. For example, a heavy meal at lunch, particularly if accompanied by a couple of alcoholic beverages, often creates lethargic aftereffects slowing down your normal rate of performance. Additionally, heavy meals consumed over an extended period of time will likely add excessive weight. And overweight people are generally less healthy than those who keep their weight within an acceptable range, and are prone to lose more time from work due to illness. In summary, then, eat lightly and save time.

20. Avoid sit-down conferences

There are times when a sit-down conference in the administrator's office is the best way to transact business, but the sit-down conference is often overused. Whenever a sit-down conference is held when a briefer method could be used to accomplish the same objective, time is wasted. There are any number of ways to communicate with people to avoid a formal face-to-face conference. In some cases, a simple note is all that is needed, or a telephone call. Where more than two people need to be involved, a conference call can be arranged. Or, if you have a speaker telephone, other people in the office can be involved in a conference even though there is only one telephone.

I try to keep people out of my office except when there is no better way to transact business. Several tactics can be employed to deter unnecessary office visits. You can meet the intruder in the doorway and not permit entry. This approach usually forces the visitor to get to the point. Or if a conference must take place, you can beat the other person to the draw. Visit their office! You will be in more control and can terminate the conference more easily than if you met in your office.

Often an administrator is accosted in a hallway. In such an event, remain in the hallway. Don't invite the accoster into your office. Or tell the person to walk with you to your destination and conduct a conference while you're walking. That will test just how serious the visitor really is. In other cases where you are travelling with others in an automobile, a conference can be held in transit.

21. Carry a note pad

How many good ideas are never used because they are forgotten? How many times have you forgotten to do something that you should have done? The best way to keep good ideas and avoid forgetting obligations is to have available at all times something to keep notes on. For many, this could be a simple and inexpensive 3" x 5" note pad. Whether a note pad, clip board, notebook or pocket recorder is used, you should have some means at all times to record thoughts which need to be retrieved later. By writing down such matters, you are freed from the burden of trying to remember ideas and obligations and freed of the worry of forgetting.

At the time of the writing of this book, I had on my desk a stack of some 500 3" x 5" file cards which contained the basic contents for another book. All of the information on these cards was recorded while I was either driving my automobile, attending a meeting, conducting a conference, watching television or engaging in some similar activity. Had these thoughts not been recorded immediately, they would have been lost forever.

Administrators who refuse to record obligations and ideas are bound to forget. Each time this happens, time is wasted because a deadline is missed or a good idea goes unused. Not only that, but administrators who refuse to carry a note pad needlessly clutter their minds with concerns which could just as easily be carried on paper.

22. Plan for found time

The average person often faces times during which there are no specific immediate requirements. Faced with such "found" time, many people will pick up some inane reading material or turn to the television set for distraction. Or if on the job, a person may either stretch out a current task or engage in some low priority activity, such as organizing the contents of the desk or purging the files. These are wasteful ways to use unanticipated time.

The best way to be prepared to use unplanned free time is to have extra projects pending at all times. You will recall that earlier in this chapter, the value of goals and objectives was stressed. By having goals and objectives on the job, you will seldom have a problem with deciding what to do with some unanticipated free time. You will immediately apply the found time to your goals and objectives.

Let's say that you have chosen as an objective the reading of three specific books by a certain date. By having one of these books in your possession at all times, you have a ready-made activity for those surprise moments when there is "nothing to do." The rule, then, for using unanticipated free time is: Always have access to some extra project which can be worked on in spare moments.

23. Skip meetings

I s there an administrator alive who has not attended some meetings which were a waste of time? Have you ever attended a meeting where the information presented could have been communicated by a memorandum? The answer to both of these questions is likely "yes." Useless meetings are very expensive to the employer and to the employee. If an employee spends only one afternoon each week in a useless meeting, the employee has lost 10% of her or his work week!

Would you be willing to have someone take away 10% of your work week and still hold you responsible for a full week of work? As far as the employer is concerned, one meeting for an afternoon for 50 people, each being paid $300 per day, costs the employer $7,500. And that does not include travel reimbursement, where travel is required to attend the meeting, or the expenses for preparing the room for the meeting and the cleanup afterwards.

Do not hold a meeting if there is a better way to accomplish the objective. By the same token, do not attend a worthless meeting if it can be avoided.

But even good meetings need not be attended. I regularly do not attend meetings and conferences if there is a more efficient way to obtain the information to be presented. The best way to avoid a meeting but still obtain the necessary information is to ask a colleague to brief you on what transpired. The briefing is usually better than the meeting itself and always takes much less time than the length of the meeting.

24. Screen mail

Some administrators receive so much mail that if they processed it all themselves, there would be little time left to accomplish their main jobs. Whether the mail is voluminous or slight, however, someone else, probably a secretary, should screen the mail. Naturally, there is no single rule which can be applied to all situations for the screening of mail; however, there are several ways that your secretary can save you time in dealing with your mail. The secretary can:

- ◆ Open the mail.
- ◆ Sort the mail into categories.
- ◆ Send some mail to the appropriate office.
- ◆ Draft responses to some letters.
- ◆ Attach backup information where needed.

Every hour spent on these activities by your secretary is one hour saved by you. One hour per day saved in this fashion is five hours per week, which is over 10% of the work week!

25. Screen appointments

Appointments are often unnecessary, and, as such, waste time. To avoid unnecessary appointments always seek a better way to handle the situation. In order to do this, however, you (or your secretary) must find out what is the exact reason for the appointment. When this information is known, an appointment may not be needed. Perhaps the matter can be handled by a brief discussion on the telephone. Or perhaps the appointment is just to obtain information—information which could be sent through the mail. Or perhaps the caller really needs to see someone else. As far as appointments are concerned, the same rule applies here as the rule for meetings: Don't agree to an appointment unless there is no better way to handle the matter for which the appointment was intended.

26. Screen readings

Many administrators receive letters, memoranda, reports, books, charts, newsletters, advertisements, notes, etc. daily. You should not read all of these materials personally. In some cases, your secretary can divert the materials to a more appropriate office. In other cases, he or she can flag the more important documents. Whatever method is used, however, you should read only those materials which contribute to accomplishing your job.

To prioritize reading material, you may wish to use the three-category method discussed previously. Category one is for reading material which must be read immediately. Category two is for materials which need to be read within a few weeks. And the last category is reserved for materials which are not required reading but should be read at some point in time.

27. Plan each day

"I'm too busy to plan" is the common complaint of the administrator who seems always behind—always a little disorganized. Such a complaint is ridiculous! The only reason that people don't have time to plan is because they don't *make* time to plan. Without a daily plan of activities, accompanied by time allotments, time will be wasted each day, and, worse, you are likely to fail at the job. In other words, *failing to plan is planning to fail!*

28. Make decisions promptly

Much time can be wasted due to slow decision making, especially where the failure to make a decision promptly affects the work of many people. A decision is an act which gives the go-ahead for action to take place. Until a decision is made, all subordinates are held in abeyance, biding their time on activities of lesser value, waiting for the boss to make up his or her mind. To the extent that a decision is delayed unnecessarily, time is wasted.

Fear and lack of information are the two major causes of indecision. Fear is usually caused by an employer who has demonstrated in many ways that mistakes, no matter how small, will bring about punishment. Fear is caused by the employer who takes good work for granted but highlights mistakes of employees. As long as fear permeates the offices where important decisions are made, few worthwhile decisions will be made. Fear stultifies the decision-making process.

If decisions are to be made to benefit the employer, there must be the freedom to make an occasional wrong decision. Babe Ruth was the home run king, but it has been alleged that he was also a strike-out king. In other words, he made a lot of bad decisions in order to achieve a lot of good results. Had he been punished for every strike, he likely would have made few home runs.

All decisions require the weighing of all relevant considerations; therefore, all information surrounding the decision should be available. Once the relevant information has been assembled, it should be arranged so that all options are known and can be compared. Some people are hesitant to make decisions until all relevant information is known and all risks have been reduced to an absolute minimum. But all needed information is not always available when a decision needs to be made. In such a situation, the best rule is: Somebody do something!

29. Resist upward delegation

Some subordinates are masters at dumping problems on their bosses. Some subordinates may attempt to appeal to the ego of their supervisors by stating: "You're so intelligent and experienced, I know you can do this better than I can." Or a subordinate may come in with a problem stating: "I don't have the authority to settle this matter so you do it." Or the subordinate may say: "We could do this, or we could do that. What do you want to do, boss?" All of these types of approaches should be resisted. No subordinate should be allowed to dump a problem on the boss without just cause.

If the employee claims the problem is too tough, point out that the employee should be able to handle it. If the employee claims lack of authority to resolve a problem, give that person the authority to do so. If the subordinate asks you what you want to do, respond with a question as to what the subordinate thinks should be done. In other words, force your subordinates to make decisions, to make recommendations, and then hold them accountable for their actions. Do not allow upward delegation. If necessary, put a sign on your desk which reads: *"Don't forget to take your problem with you."*

30. Seize the initiative

The overriding value of long-range goals and short-range objectives has already been discussed. By developing such goals and objectives, you have taken the first and most important step toward using time wisely. Once goals and objectives are set, action must, of necessity, follow if those targets are to be met. In other words, you must take the initiative to reach desired goals. This means to "stay ahead of the power curve." By seizing the initiative, you have a better control over how time is to be spent than would be the case if waiting for others to make all the decisions. Those who wait to be told what to do are people who have lost control over the time available. And, by losing control over how time is to be used, you lose the opportunity to save time. But, more importantly, any administrator who falls behind the power curve is an administrator who is loosing control of his or her job.

31. Know where to look

One of the major functions of an administrator is to collect information in order to make decisions and complete projects. Some place in the world there is enough information to solve any problem or make any decision. The challenge is how to get the information when it is needed, because not knowing where or how to get information not only wastes time, but it can cause wrong decisions to be made.

Dictionaries, encyclopedias, libraries and the yellow pages of the telephone directory are obvious and common sources of information needed on a regular basis. But, you must learn to use far more sources of information than these elementary ones. Information is located all around us, and, by exercising tenacity and creativity, you will find it while others fail.

I once needed a very selective mailing list but was told by all experts that such a list did not exist. However, after a number of persistent telephone calls and letters, I found that the needed addresses existed in a computer memory of a federal agency. Since the information was public, a request was made for the information and the valuable list was produced for a cost of slightly less than $1,000. The same list, even if it existed elsewhere, could not have been purchased for less than five times that amount. To repeat, the rule for getting hard information is to be persistent and creative.

32. Use experts

One way to obtain needed information in order to make decisions quickly or to accomplish tasks on time is to call upon the experts. There is an expert someplace on just about any topic. All you need to do is search, and the needed expert will appear. Administrators are seldom experts in all of the fields they must administer, and effective administrators learn early in their careers to rely upon the experts to obtain needed information in order to make decisions.

Good experts are very cost efficient. They are paid a specific fee to deliver a specific service. They require no desk or administrative overhead, fringe benefits or grievance procedures. And they can be fired anytime their work is unacceptable.

33. Know how to close

Every conference, every appointment and every telephone call must come to an end sooner or later, and, preferably, sooner. But many such encounters continue long after they should have ended because some administrators don't know how to bring about closure. Here are some suggestions to help bring discussions to a close at the appropriate time:

- At the beginning of the meeting, announce the time limit for the discussion.
- When you have achieved all that is wanted from a discussion, summarize the meeting.
- Don't introduce any topic unrelated to the subject under discussion.
- Have an understanding with your secretary that he or she should enter your office if a meeting goes too long to remind you that you have other obligations to turn to.
- Announce to visitors that they have five minutes remaining to say what needs to be said.
- Say, "Are there any final points which need to be made before we conclude this meeting?"

When two or more people engage in a business discussion, the objective should be to transact all needed business in the shortest time possible. The effective administrator will employ many tactics to achieve that objective.

34. Learn to speed read

How much of your day is spent reading? How many times are you given material to read while being asked questions simultaneously? Research indicates that administrators spend an average of 10 to 20 hours per week reviewing written materials. Wouldn't it be nice if their reading time could be reduced? Even a 10% reduction would release one to two hours per week. Chances are that any of the reputable commercial or academic reading acceleration courses would improve reading speed and comprehension by more than 10%. Such courses are relatively inexpensive and widely available.

Two or three hours in reading saved each week may not sound like a significant amount of time, but this savings, coupled with the other suggestions in this book, should add up to a considerable amount of time.

35. Reverse Parkinson's Law

The British economist C. Parkinson propounded a number of satirical statements expressed as economic laws. His most famous one is: "Work expands to fill the time allotted to it." There is a great deal of truth to this "law," especially in bureaucracies where there is limited ability to hold bureaucrats personally responsible for production.

An effective way to save a significant amount of time is to reverse Parkinson's Law by requiring that "work shrink to fill the time allotted to it." By placing a time limit on assignments, time is automatically saved, for without a deadline, tasks go on and on, wasting time. When a subordinate is given less time than that person would like to complete a task, it is surprising how often the deadline is met, despite protestations from the employee.

The use of deadlines to force the wise use of time has been discussed elsewhere in this book, but, in the context of Parkinson's Law, it is being suggested here that deadlines are not enough. In addition to imposing deadlines, the amount of time allotted to tasks should be carefully limited. By doing this, time can be released to accomplish tasks which otherwise might go undone.

36. Avoid eye contact

Much has been written concerning the significance of eye contact, with most experts suggesting that eye contact is imperative in face-to-face discussions. Granted, eye contact plays an important role in effective communication when used properly; however, in my view, most experts overstress the importance and significance of eye contact. Constant eye contact can actually create unnecessary and unwanted tension in some situations.

As far as saving time is concerned, though, eye contact can be an important issue, since eye contact is often the first connection prior to a face-to-face discussion. Therefore, if discussion with another person is not wanted, then avoid eye contact. For administrators who do not have private offices, the chance of eye contact can be minimized by situating the desk in a manner so that you face away from passing pedestrian traffic. Not surprisingly, however, most people with desks seem to place them in a manner that maximizes the chance of eye contact with passersby. Consequently, every casual passerby (especially the casual ones) and visitor becomes a potential time waster because once eye contact is made, there is an implied invitation to open a discussion.

37. Learn to write faster

I maintain multiple offices, one of which is in my home. All these offices contain a personal word processor. Granted, not everyone can type, and not every administrator needs to type. But, for some, the ability to use a typewriter or word processor well is a significant advantage in saving time. For one thing, a skilled typist can type faster than the average person can hand write. Also, the typewritten page is more easily read, and that saves time for you as well. Additionally, some text does not lend itself readily to dictation but, rather, requires careful analysis as it is being written. A typewriter is ideal for this type of composition. Furthermore, as far as my life style is concerned, there are many times when a secretary is not immediately available. Consequently, a personal typewriter readily available becomes very helpful, particularly for material which is not easily dictated into a tape recorder.

There are many occasions when you must take notes rapidly. In such cases, shorthand is very helpful; however, few administrators have such a skill. But there is a way that anyone can learn to increase the speed of her or his own handwriting through the use of "speed writing." This procedure, advertised in many popular magazines, is a common sense method of shortening words by replacing words with numbers, by deleting consonants and by using standard abbreviations. According to this method, the sentence, "You, too, can easily see the president on Wednesday for a short period without an appointment," would appear as follows: "U,2, cn ezly c th pres on Wed 4 a shrt pd w/o an apntmt." At first try, the method may appear awkward, but with practice it becomes quite natural—and it does save time!

38. Reduce sleep

On the average, people sleep about 3,000 hours per year, or one-third of their lives. Some people do not need eight hours of sleep each night. For those people, any sleep in excess of eight hours should be considered a potential waste of time. Just think, if you could reduce the need for sleep by only one hour per night, you would find 365 hours per year; and 365 hours is equivalent to ten work weeks or two and one-half months on the job!

Almost everybody can reduce their need for sleep to some extent without any deleterious health trade-off if they are willing to follow these simple rules:

- Keep constructively busy and interested in life.
- Engage in enjoyable and light exercise regularly.
- Eat natural food, and eat lightly.
- Maintain a happy and peaceful state of mind.
- Sleep in a good bed in a quiet, well-ventilated room.
- Learn to "cat nap" at least once a day. Or develop the ability to relax through meditation.
- Have something enjoyable to look forward to each day.

Try these simple rules and begin to reduce your sleep by a few minutes each night until you attain a reduction of one hour. In some cases you may find that changing the hours of sleep may lessen the need for sleep. For example, some people find that by going to bed one hour earlier than customary, they can rise an hour and a half earlier the next morning, thus, shortening the sleep period by 30 minutes.

39. Timing

There is a best time to undertake any task. Some tasks should be done immediately, while others should be put off. There is no simple rule, however, to make the distinction noted here. Each case must be analyzed on its own merits. In some cases, the decision on timing of task accomplishment is based on intuition, and, in other cases, timing may be dictated by overriding events. Regardless, every task should be approached with the question: "When is the best time to do this?" In some cases, protracted procrastination may be the best answer because some problems simply go away without any action. However, more often than not, the answer to when to do the job is "Now!"

40. Monitor results — not activities

Every employee should have a specific job to perform and every employee should be evaluated primarily on how well she or he performs that job. Unfortunately, in too many instances, especially in government bureaucracies where personal accountability is diffused, employees are evaluated on factors of questionable relevance to their jobs, such as personality traits. In too many instances, the evaluation of employees is unfairly influenced by whether or not their supervisors like them.

The failure to evaluate employees on the basis of an objective evaluation of their job performance breeds sycophantism and directs time and energy to activities not directly contributory to the mission of the agency. By evaluating the activities of employees, rather than the results of their activities, you can waste your own time, as well as misdirect employees into believing that results are not what counts.

Not only should you concentrate on the job results of your subordinates, but you should keep your eyes clearly focused on your own goals and disengage yourself from activities which do not contribute to achieving those goals. By stressing results for yourself and your subordinates, you are able to save much time because extraneous activity is quickly eliminated in a task-oriented work environment.

41. The forty-first rule

There is an important 41st rule, without which all the others are rendered moot. You must exercise at least as much care in your choice of a secretary as the school board would in selecting a superintendent. In order for the foregoing rules to work, you must have a secretary who can walk on water, juggle eggs and smooth boiling oil without singeing a hair. Your secretary must remain unruffled in a hurricane and retain composure when all others are losing theirs and blaming it on your secretary. Your secretary must be unfailingly sensitive to the feelings of others, but expect no support or even remote interest when the world threatens to crumble around his or her ears. Your secretary must be willing to lie convincingly for you without ever losing integrity. Your secretary must be willing to work long hours at tasks you are incapable of doing for pay you would find laughable. Your secretary must never feel insulted when those who are her or his mental inferiors refer to her or him as "just a secretary." Your secretary must be mentor, confidante, conspirator, scapegoat, watchdog, ferret, workhorse and bodyguard.

The Ultimate Secret

T his book has offered over 60 effective ways to "save" time. Most of the tactics discussed should be of immediate practicality to any administrator who wishes to save time, irrespective of the job. As we have learned from this book, time cannot be "saved." All we can do is learn to use effectively the little time available to us. Therefore, much of time "saving" is really based on how we wish to spend our time personally and professionally. For example, the decision to watch television at home some evening, rather than to exercise, is a conscious or subconscious choice based upon some priority. The decision to eat lunch in the office, rather than join the gang at the local restaurant, is also a decision based upon some priority, even though the priority may not be of conscious awareness.

In all cases where we make a choice as to how to spend time, we make a decision based upon some apparent or hidden priority. The decision as to how time will be spent is made on the basis of whether or not it contributes to what we want, what we are after. Which leads us to the first ultimate secret for "saving" time, which is: *Decide what you want to do with your life personally and professionally.*

You cannot make wise decisions as to how to use the fixed amount of time available to you unless you know where you are going personally and professionally. You cannot use time wisely unless you have goals in your professional life. The supreme time waster is the failure to have such goals for your life. Without such goals, we may as well let others tell us what to do or flip a coin. Without goals, we go willy-nilly through life directed by any person who wishes to exploit us, or buffeted by any event which enters our lives.

So, the first super rule for saving time is: *Choose your life goals.*

However, I would be less than honest to say that the selection of life goals is easy. Take a few minutes without reading further and contemplate just how you wish to spend the rest of your life. Try to identify just what it is that you are after in your life. Think seriously about this for a few minutes.

Here are some typical responses to the question, "What are your goals in life?" which I have posed to my seminar audiences:

- Happiness.
- More money.
- Security.
- A big house.
- A long life.
- Good health.
- A better job.
- A family.

But frankly, these goals, by themselves, don't mean much. For example, what is "happiness"? Try to define what happiness means to you. When you have done that, try to determine how you go about achieving happiness.

Why would you want "more money"? Money in itself is meaningless. It's only what money can do that counts. So what do you want to use more money for? Will these things which you obtain with more money lead you toward your life goals?

What is "security"? Although many people view security as a material thing, that is, a good job, retirement protection, etc., security for some is more a state of mind, having little to do with material things.

Why do you want a "big house"? Is the big house really a symptom of a deeper need or a statement of pride? Is the big house really a goal in life, or is it merely a step toward a more important goal?

What does "good health" mean? Is it the ability to run a mile in four minutes, or is it the absence of pain? Why do you want good health? To be free of discomfort or to have strength to accomplish a more important goal?

What is a "better job"? And why would you want a better job? Isn't the desire for a better job really a statement that you want a better job for some higher need?

Some young people will state that marriage and a family are their goal. But marriage and a family are likely not ends in themselves. Besides, some marriages and families are a catastrophe so that possibility should be considered when you thinks of marriage and family as goals.

The point being made here is that although goal selection is the foundation for using time wisely, goal setting, if done properly, is a difficult and excruciating process, and it's not enough simply to say that your goal in life is to be "happy". Goals must be carefully defined and understood. But once goal setting has been conquered, there is a tremendous sense of purpose and peace given to your life.

Incidentally, goal setting is not a onetime process. It is a process which you may consciously initiate at some specific point in your life, but it is also a process which should continue throughout life. As you change, and as events around the you change, modifications must be made in your life goals; otherwise, you may find yourself pursuing goals no longer of value.

Once goals have been selected, it's time to take the second ultimate step, which is using wisely what little time is left in your life. That second critical step is: *Take charge of your life personally and professionally.*

You cannot achieve your goals in life if you allow others to exploit you and allow events to control you. Once goals have been set, you must seize the initiative for controlling your life. This means that a plan must be laid out which leads to the fulfillment of the selected goals.

Keep in mind that most administrators will have a tendency to divide their goals into two categories: personal goals and professional goals. This is not to suggest that the two categories are unrelated, however. As a matter of fact, the happy person is often one whose personal life and professional life work together to fulfill overall life goals. Most people who go through a serious goal-setting procedure will attempt to define their ultimate goals first, and then will attempt to make their professional goals consistent with their personal and more ultimate goals.

Let's hypothesize that a teacher has chosen goals of achieving professional excellence and a happy secure family life. Let's further assume that this teacher (right or wrong) has decided that becoming a superintendent of a large school district would represent the achievement of excellence in the education profession. Given that goal, the teacher should begin to define what conditions lead to a superintendency. Once the teacher has determined what conditions are most likely to lead to a superintendency, those conditions or the situations to make those conditions possible should be vigorously sought.

For example, such a person should obtain certification in school administration, preferably with a doctorate. Furthermore, an attempt should be made to gain varied administrative experience. Often smaller school districts provide a greater opportunity for such experiences. When the teacher feels ready for a superintendency, a carefully planned campaign should be embarked upon to contact those school districts where vacancies exist. Naturally, there is no guarantee that this strategy will result in a superintendency. But one thing is certain, if the teacher does not at least try this strategy, that person definitely will not become a superintendent.

The other goal of this mythical teacher was to have a happy and secure family life. It is likely in this hypothetical case that the teacher (right or wrong) has decided that a well-paying job as a superintendent would contribute to the care and security of the family. Whether or not subsequent events would indicate that a superintendency helped that person to achieve a happy and secure family is an issue answered only by the passage of time and events. The point is, nevertheless, that this person has chosen definite goals and has set about to develop a strategy to achieve those goals.

Let's assume further that this teacher, in an effort to build a happy and secure family, has decided that every weekend at least part of one day would be spent in some enjoyable activity which the entire family can engage in. This commitment, then, becomes part of a strategy which makes the family activity the number one priority for each weekend. As a result, the choice as to how to spend time over the weekend has been narrowed somewhat. Specifically, time is spent each weekend on an activity which contributes directly to the teacher's goal of happiness and security for the family.

In conclusion, then, the two super rules for saving time are:

- Decide what you want to do with your life, and
- Take charge of your life.

About the Author

D r. Richard G. Neal is a career educator, who has taught from the elementary to the college graduate level. He has served in many educational management and consultant positions, both in the public and private sectors. Active in various publications, Dr. Neal is the author of numerous books and many articles in the areas of personnel administration, labor relations and school management. Additionally, he has served as editor of several national newsletters. His books, *School Based Management: A Detailed Guide for Successful Implementation*, *School Based Management: A Training Guide for Site Committees*, *School Based Management: The Final Examination* and *Site Committee Training* are practical bibles on how to do it.

Over an extended period of time, Dr. Neal has been an active consultant for school boards and school administrators throughout the United States and Canada, having made presentations in over 300 seminars and conferences. He has been a featured speaker for the Association of School Business Officials International, the National School Boards Association, the Association of School Administrators, the National Clearinghouse on School Based Management, the National Academy for School Executives, the Sage Education Corporation, dozens of state and regional associations of school boards and administrators, as well as a long list of individual school districts and private organizations.

Dr. Neal is currently the president of Educational Satellite Training, Inc. (EdSaTra, Inc.), which specializes in long distance learning by satellite.